**Bromley** **Beckenham Library**

020 8650 7292
Please return/renew this item
by the last date shown.
Books may also be renewed by
phone and Internet.

# Simple Machines

# Levers

by Martha E. H. Rustad

raintree

a Capstone company — publishers for children

Raintree is an imprint of Capstone Global Library Limited, a company incorporated in England and Wales having its registered office at 264 Banbury Road, Oxford, OX2 7DY – Registered company number: 6695582

**www.raintree.co.uk**
myorders@raintree.co.uk

Edited by Marissa Kirkman
Designed by Kyle Grentz (cover) and Charmaine Whitman (interior)
Original illustrations © Capstone Global Library Limited 2018
Picture research by Jo Miller
Production by Katy LaVigne
Originated by Capstone Global Library Limited
Printed and bound in India.

ISBN 978 1 4747 5359 3
21 20 19 18 17
10 9 8 7 6 5 4 3 2 1

**British Library Cataloguing in Publication Data**
A full catalogue record for this book is available from the British Library.

**Acknowledgements**
We would like to thank the following for permission to reproduce photographs: Capstone Studio: Karon Dubke, 19; iStockphoto: asiseeit, 13, Image Source, 5, kall9, 11, stigmatize, 15; Shutterstock: 3445128471, 20, Andris Tkacenko, 17 (bottom), Anneka, 24, Kristina Postnikova, cover, 1, Shcherbakov Ilya, 7, Syda Productions, 17 (top), Volcko Mar, 9, wavebreakmedia, 21

Every effort has been made to contact copyright holders of material reproduced in this book. Any omissions will be rectified in subsequent printings if notice is given to the publisher.

# Contents

# Levers help

Work is hard!

We need help.

Use a simple machine.

These tools help us work.

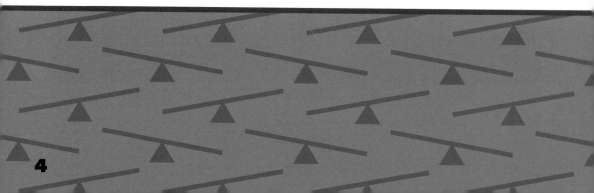

lever

A lever helps us lift.

A lever helps move loads.

lever

# How levers work

A lever is a bar.

It sits on a point.

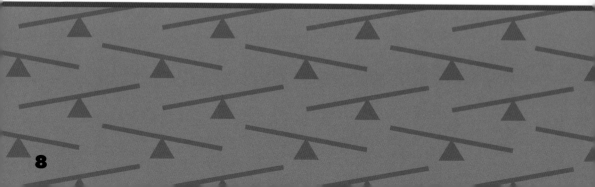

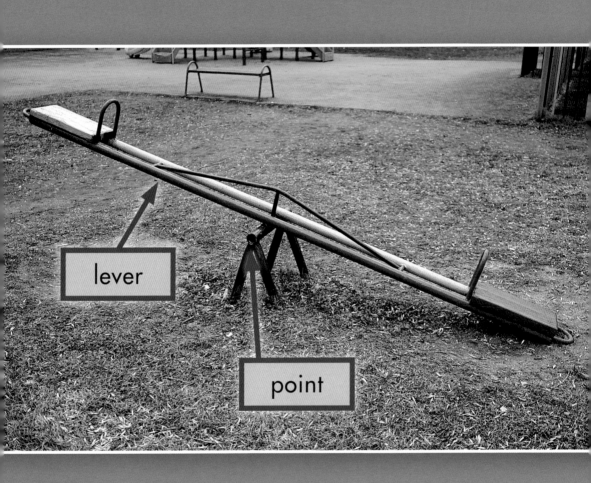

lever

point

Push down on a lever.

The other side moves up.

lever

Put a big load on
one end of the lever.
Push down.
Lift the load!

lever

load

# Everyday levers

A see-saw is a lever.

Push!

A friend goes up.

You go down.

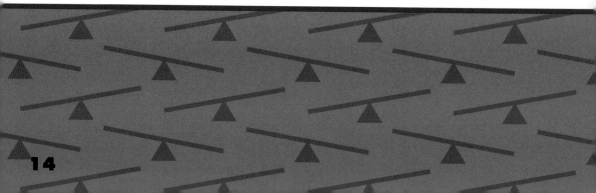

A hammer is a lever.

Pull!

A nail comes out.

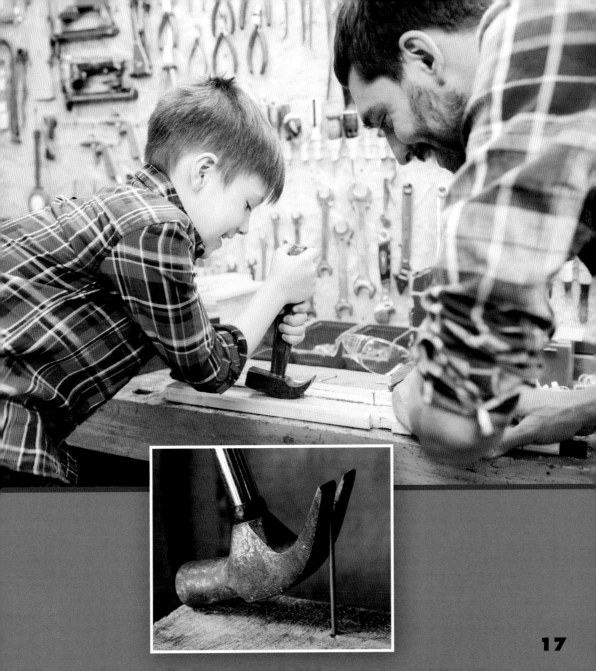

Scissors are levers.

Squeeze!

The paper is cut.

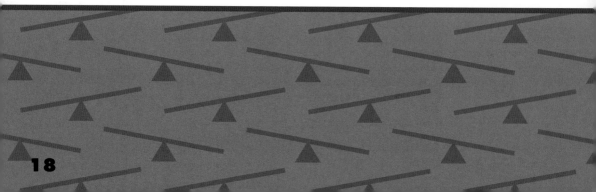

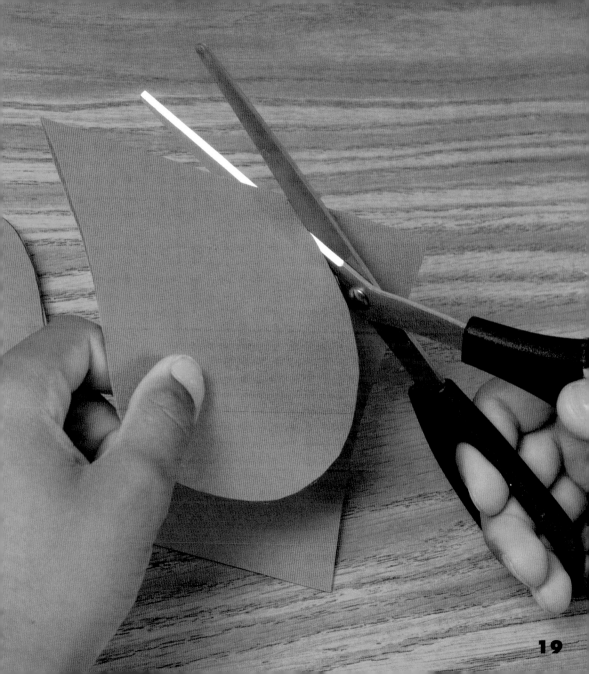

We use a simple machine.

It makes work easier and fun.

lever

# Glossary

**bar**  long, stiff stick or flat block

**lever**  bar that you can use to lift a load by putting one end under the load and pushing down on the other end; a lever is a simple machine

**load**  object that you want to move or lift

**point**  end or tip of an object; a lever turns on a point called a fulcrum

**scissors**  tool used to cut paper; scissors are two levers stuck together

**simple machine**  tool that makes it easier to move something

**work**  job that must be done

# Read more

*Fred Flintstone's Adventures with Levers: Lift that Load!* (Flintstones Explain Simple Machines), Mark Weakland (Capstone Press, 2016)

*Making Machines with Levers* (Simple Machine Projects), Chris Oxlade (Raintree, 2016)

*The Kids' Book of Simple Machines: Cool Projects and Activities That Make Science Fun*, Kelly Doudna (Mighty Media Kids, 2015)

# Websites

www.bbc.co.uk/guides/zptckqt#zgb7xnb
Explore forces and simple machines with Seymour on the BBC website.

www.rigb.org/index.php?url=%2Ffamilies%2Fexperim ental%2Ffor-5-8-year-olds
Investigate science at home with simple experiments on The Royal Institution's website for children.

# Comprehension questions

1. What does a lever sit on?

2. What happens when you push down on one side of a lever?

3. Have you ever used a lever? How did it help you?

# Index